★ IT'S MY STATE! ★
Oregon

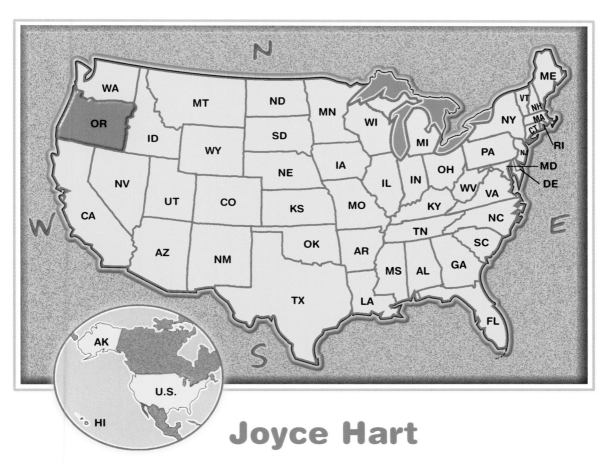

Joyce Hart

Marshall Cavendish
Benchmark
New York

Marshall Cavendish Benchmark
99 White Plains Road
Tarrytown, New York 10591-9001
www.marshallcavendish.us

Library of Congress Cataloging-in-Publication Data

Hart, Joyce, 1954-
Oregon / by Joyce Hart.
p. cm. — (It's my state!)
Summary: "Surveys the history, geography, economy, and people of
Oregon"—Provided by publisher.
Includes index.
ISBN 0-7614-1908-X

1. Oregon—Juvenile literature. I. Title. II. Series.
F876.3.H37 2006   979.5—dc22   2005018063

Photo research by Candlepants, Inc.

Front cover: Bananastock/PictureQuest
Back cover illustration: The license plate shows Oregon's postal abbreviation, followed by its year of statehood.

The photographs in this book are used by permission and through the courtesy of: *Corbis:* 37, 38, 41 (bottom), 52; Bettmann, 41 (top), 50 (top), 51 (bottom), 51 (top); Patrick Johns, 4 (bottom); Steve Terrill, 8; Craig Tuttle, 9, 12, 72; Gary Braasch, 10, 11, 15, 40; Phil Schermeister, 13, 54, 57; William Manning, 18, 72 (middle); Larry Neubauer, 14; Galen Rowell, 19; Brandon D. Cole, 23 (bottom); Underwood & Underwood, 24; Charles E. Rotkin, 39; James L. Amos, 44; Kevin R. Morris, 46, 49; Warren Morgan, 53; Philip James Corwin, 55; Maiman Rick / Corbis Sygma, 51(middle); Brooks Craft, 50 (middle); Reuters, 50 (bottom); Owaki-Kulla, 73 (top). *Northwind Picture Archives:* 26, 31, 34, 35, 36. *Animals Animals / Earth Scenes:* Michael Gadomski, 4 (top); Erwin & Peggy Bauer, 21, 22 (top); Phyllis Greenberg, 22 (bottom); Zigmund Leszczynski, 23 (middle). *Visuals Unlimited:* Leroy Simon, 5 (top). *Minden Pictures:* Jim Brandenburg, 5 (middle), 22 (middle); Michael Quinton, 5 (bottom). *Picture Quest:* Brand X Pictures, 66, 68; Index Stock, 71, 73 (bottom). *SuperStock:* age fotostock, 17, 70; David Falconer, 42, 57; Richard Cummins, 58; Steve Vidler, 62. *Envision:* George Mattei, 4 (middle), 23 (top), 72 (top), 73 (middle); Steven Needham, 69. *Oregon Historical Society OrHi93065:* 28.

Book design by Anahid Hamparian
Printed in Malaysia

1   3   5   6   4   2

Contents

A Quick Look at Oregon

Nickname: The Beaver State
Population: 3,594,586 (2004 estimate)
Statehood: February 14, 1859

Tree: **Douglas Fir**

The Douglas fir, which can grow well over 300 feet and as straight as arrow in Oregon's forests, was selected as the state tree in 1939. This evergreen tree was named for David Douglas, a man from Scotland who was sent to the United States to study it. Wood from the Douglas fir is often used in constructing houses because of its strength, which is said to be as hardy as concrete.

Fruit: **Pear**

In 2005, the Oregon state legislature made the pear the state fruit. Pears are Oregon's most important tree-fruit crop. Oregon orchards grow a variety of pears from Bosc to Bartlett to Anjou. These tasty fruits are shipped throughout country and around the world.

Flower: **Oregon Grape**

In 1899, Oregon adopted the Oregon grape as its state flower. Many other flowers had been considered, but this distinctive evergreen bush, which produces small bell-shaped yellow flowers in the spring and blue berries in the fall, was determined to be the favorite. It is found all over the state, but it grows best along the Pacific Coast.

Insect: Oregon Swallowtail Butterfly

Swallowtail butterflies are common on the East Coast, but the only kind that lives west of the Missouri River is the Oregon swallowtail. With black and yellow markings, the adult female measures about 4 inches from wing tip to wing tip. These butterflies prefer dry weather, so the best place to look for them is east of the Cascades, especially along the cliffs of the Columbia River.

Bird: Western Meadowlark

The western meadowlark is recognized by its bright yellow chest and black V-shaped collar. This bird is only about 9 inches long, so it might be hard to find. It might be easier to listen for its song, which sounds like someone playing a flute from a high note down to a low note. The meadowlark spends a lot of time on the ground, but when it does fly, it flaps its wings several times, then sails for a few seconds with its wings held still.

Animal: Beaver

The beaver was almost completely wiped out of Oregon's woodlands by fur trappers. Nowadays, the beaver is protected by laws. Beavers can be found along many of Oregon's rivers and are often called nature's engineers, because of their ability to build complex dams that help to protect riverbanks from being washed away. The beaver is also Oregon State University's mascot.

OREGON

Astoria

Mount Hood

Milton-Freewater

PACIFIC OCEAN

The Dalles

COLUMBIA RIVER

HELLS CANYON NATIONAL RECREATION AREA

STATE OF OREGON 1859

Portland

DESCHUTES RIVER

Pendleton

JOHN DAY RIVER

BLUE MOUNTAINS

La Grande

SNAKE RIVER

Salem

CASCADE RANGE

DESCHUTES NATIONAL FOREST

WALLOWA MOUNTAINS

Albany

WILLAMETTE NATIONAL FOREST

UMATILLA NATIONAL FOREST

Baker City

Corvallis

WILLAMETTE RIVER

Bend

Redmond

Eugene

UMPQUA RIVER

Ontario

Coos Bay

COAST RANGES

Roseburg

NEWBERRY NATIONAL VOLCANIC MONUMENT

Burns

MALHEUR LAKE

LAKE OWYHEE

ROGUE RIVER

CRATER LAKE

Alkali Lake

OWYHEE RIVER

Jordan Valley

SISKIYOU NATIONAL FOREST

UPPER KLAMATH LAKE

FREEMONT NATIONAL FOREST

Brookings

Grants Pass

Medford

Klamath Falls

Lakeview

HART MOUNTAIN NATIONAL ANTELOPE REFUGE

N
W   E
S

1 The Beaver State

People who live in Oregon, the tenth-largest state, enjoy a wide variety of land regions. These include rain forests, hot and dry deserts, sand dune beaches, and mountains topped with ice and snow. In between Oregon's two major mountain ranges is a large green valley, where most Oregonians make their homes.

Oregon is rectangular in shape, and is about 400 miles wide and almost 300 hundred miles long. If you were to begin a trip at the western shoreline, starting about midway down the coast, you would first travel across the Coast Range Mountains. Moving eastward, you would wander through the wide green Willamette Valley before climbing the highest elevations in the state at the Cascade Mountains. Once you reach the

Oregon's Borders
North: Washington
South: California and Nevada
East: Idaho
West: Pacific Ocean

eastern side of the Cascades, the air turns very dry. The landscape changes from thickly-treed forests to mostly open plains. A large portion of the eastern side of the state is home to many large farms. Along the eastern border of the state, is the Blue Mountain

Range, a place where gold mining was
once very popular.

*From river to mountain to coast,
Oregon's landscape is diverse and
breathtaking.*

Natural Forces

Some of Oregon's major land formations began about 200 million years
ago as the North American continent
and the floor of the Pacific Ocean started bumping into one another. Scientists
say that the Earth's surface is made up
of a 60-mile-thick outer layer that is
broken into many pieces, which they
call plates. These plates move very
slowly, some only 2 inches each year.
When two plates bump into each other,
one plate sometimes slides under the
other one. This is what happened to the land that is now
Oregon's western shore. The ocean plate sunk under the coastline, and the land on the coast was pushed upward, and the
Coast Range Mountains were created.

As the ocean plate moved under the continent, the rock
material that made up the ocean plate became very hot, melted,
and turned into lava. The lava eventually rushed to the surface.
After many explosions of lava, a line of volcanoes was created.
These volcanoes make up Oregon's Cascade Mountains.

Weather also helped to create some of the other physical features of Oregon. Moist air, blowing from the ocean released heavy
rainfall on the western slopes of the Coast Range and the Cascades. This water flowed down the mountainsides in the form of
rivers. These rivers fed the land and helped to produce a thick

growth of small plants and trees. By the time the air moved past the top of the Cascades to the eastern side of the state, it was drained of moisture, so it blew hot and dry. This is why eastern Oregon has dry desert-like conditions.

The Western Coast

The western boundary of Oregon is one of the most scenic shorelines in the world. In some places, the Coast Range Mountains rise straight up from the Pacific Ocean. In other places along the coast, there are sandy beaches. More than twenty-two rivers flow out of the Coast Range and into the ocean, creating estuaries, which are the mouths of rivers where they meet the ocean. In these estuaries, a wide range of wildlife can be found. The Columbia River estuary is the largest estuary and is located at the northernmost point of Oregon's ocean coast. In the middle of the Coast Range Mountains is Siuslaw National Forest, a large rainforest.

There are small towns along the coast such as Astoria, in the north. Florence, with its long sandy beaches, is a popular tourist town located at the middle of the coast. At the southern end of Oregon's ocean shoreline is Brookings. It is located in what is sometimes referred to as the Banana Belt of Oregon because of the mild winters that occur there.

Starfish cling to rocks on a sandy beach at Ecola State Park. Oregon's coastline is a favorite spot for residents and visitors.

The Willamette Valley

The Willamette Valley lies between the Coast Range, to the west, and the Cascade Mountains, to the east. At the northernmost point of the valley, are Portland and Oregon City. At the southern end of the valley is Eugene, the state's second-largest city. The Willamette River moves from south to north through this valley. It is one of the few rivers in the United States that flows in this northerly direction.

When pioneers first crossed the high Cascade Mountains and entered Willamette Valley, many of them thought they had reached a garden paradise. With the valley's beautiful trees and many wild fruit-bearing bushes, the valley looked like a great place to make a home. The soil was very fertile, which meant it was good for growing crops and the weather was neither too hot nor

The Willamette River runs through the valley near Newberg. The land in the Willamette Valley is ideal for growing different crops.

Corvallis is one of Oregon's busy, well-populated cities. It is also the home of Oregon State University.

too cold. Many different crops are grown in Willamette Valley, including mint, grass seeds, pumpkins, and corn. Today, nearly two million Oregonians live in Willamette Valley. The cities in this region include Portland, which is Oregon's largest city, Salem, Corvallis, and Eugene.

Some believe the Willamette River was named by Kalapuya Native Americans, who called it the *Wal-lamt,* which means "green river." Later, in 1826, when explorer David Douglas recorded his visit to the Pacific Northwest, he changed the spelling of the name to "Willamette."

The Cascade Mountains

Oregon's highest elevations are found in the Cascade Mountains. Mount Hood, located east of Portland, is the state's highest point. Mount Hood is more than 11,000 feet high. Other giant peaks include Mount Jefferson and the triple peaks of the Three Sisters. These large mountains are snow-capped all year round. The Cascade Range stretches from northern California to British Columbia in Canada and includes more than a dozen active volcanoes. Eruptions in Oregon, however, are infrequent. Mount Hood was the last to erupt, but that was more than two hundred years ago.

Crater Lake, located in the southern Oregon Cascades, was created when an ancient volcano, called Mount Mazama, exploded and then collapsed. It created a deep depression, or hole, which eventually filled with water. The lake is almost

Oregonians living on the farms and homes in the Hood River Valley can see Mount Hood along the horizon, rising up toward the sky.

Young hikers travel along the edge of Crater Lake.

2,000 feet deep. It is the deepest lake in the United States and is the seventh-deepest lake in the world. In the winter, the area around the lake sometimes receives more than 500 inches of snow. Each year, the melted snow and spring rain replenish the lake's water supply.

During the winter of 1950, Crater Lake National Park received the largest amount of snow Oregon has ever experienced. Storms dropped over 900 inches of snow on the area.

There are no large cities in the Cascades, but there are many communities that were built around the logging mills in the region. The Cascades provide much of Oregon's lumber.

The Eastern High Desert

More than half of the state lies on the eastern side of the Cascade Mountains. Large ranches and farms stretch over this region where cattle are raised and most of the state's wheat is grown. This is an area of few towns, but a lot of wide-open spaces.

The Blue Mountains are located on the easternmost border of this region. During the gold rush of the 1890s, many people came to this part of Oregon in search of gold. Some of the towns, such as John Day and Baker City, were established by gold miners and business owners. Also found in the northeastern corner of the state is Hells Canyon, the deepest, river-cut gorge in the United States. It is almost 8,000 feet deep, which is even deeper than the Grand Canyon. The Wallowa Mountains are also found in this region.

The Climate

Because of Oregon's variety of land formations, the weather can be very different from region to another. People who live along the western coast often experience cool summers and mild winters. Storms drop a lot of rain on the Coast Range Mountains.

The Snake River cuts through Hells Canyon, along the Oregon-Idaho border.

Winter snow is not uncommon in certain parts of the state. This farmhouse and orchard near Hillsboro have been covered by a recent snowfall.

Willamette Valley also receives a steady supply of rain from fall until spring, but the summers are usually dry and hot. Only an occasional winter storm passes over the valley, barely dropping more than a couple of inches of snow. Most of the snow that falls in Oregon lands in the Cascade Mountains, where skiing is a popular sport. Many of the tallest mountains in the Cascades receive a snowfall of 100 inches or more. Eastern Oregon receives the least rainfall, but the people who live in this

The lowest temperature ever recorded in Oregon was in Prineville in 1898 when the temperature dropped to minus 54 degrees Fahrenheit. The highest temperature occurred in Pendleton during that same year, when the thermometer reached 119 degrees Fahrenheit.

region experience some of the hottest and some of the coldest temperatures that Oregon offers.

Bodies of Water

Many people who live outside of Oregon may believe that the whole state gets a lot of rain. However, the truth is that there are cities in Oregon that do not receive as much rain as some places on the East Coast. For example, New York City receives about 47 inches of precipitation a year, while Portland receives only 36 inches. But there are places in Oregon that get a lot more rain. Laurel Mountain, one of Oregon's wettest places, recorded an amazing 204 inches of rain in 1996.

All of this rain and snow is responsible for most of Oregon's rivers, streams, and waterfalls. The water from these sources provides drinking water for humans and wildlife, but it also supplies electricity (through a series of dams), a means of transportation, and a lot of recreational fun. The main rivers of Oregon include the Columbia River, which defines most of the northern boundary between Oregon and Washington. The Willamette River runs for more than 200 miles between Portland and Eugene. Other major rivers include the John Day River in eastern Oregon and the Klamath River, which lies in the south-central portion of the state. The highest waterfall in Oregon is Mult-nomah Falls. At 628 feet, Multnomah Falls is the second-tallest waterfall in the United States.

The deep snow packs in the mountains feed the many lakes found in Oregon. Crater Lake is the deepest lake in the state, and Wallowa Lake in eastern Oregon is famous for its clear water. Some lakes in southeastern Oregon are surprisingly salty and completely dry up in the summer months.

There is also the Pacific Ocean, which hugs Oregon's entire western boundary. Although the waters of the ocean are often too cold for swimming, Oregonians love to walk along the shore, get their feet wet in the waves, and hunt for shells along the beach.

Wildlife

Nearly half of Oregon is covered in thick forests of cedar, fir, pines, and spruce trees. Before the pioneers came to Oregon, the land was filled with thick ancient forests, with some of the trees reaching heights of 400 feet or more. Only about 10 percent of old-growth forests—which are forests that have not been recently replanted—remain today. Some of the

A footbridge provides a fantastic view of Multnomah Falls.

best places to see these old-growth forests are at Oregon Caves National Monument, outside of Cave Junction in southern Oregon; at Union Creek, not far from Crater Lake; the Three Sisters Wilderness area in central Oregon; and at Lost Lake in Mount Hood National Forest.

Oregon also has a lot of wild berries. Blackberry bushes are so numerous and grow so quickly that some people consider them pests, because they are so hard to get rid of. Salmonberry, huckleberry, marionberry, and thimbleberry are other types of delicious berries that grow wild in Oregon.

The soil in this thriving forest is moist enough to support a variety of ferns.

There are many different kinds of ferns that like the wet ground in Oregon. Woods fern and maidenhair are two types. The horsetail also grows in Oregon's moist soils. It springs up from the earth looking a little like asparagus, but eventually opens its needlelike spines along its top, giving it the appearance of a horse's tail. The damp forests also provide a fertile environment for mosses, lichen, and mushrooms.

Among Oregon's many animals is a small, mouse-like critter called a vole. Voles are one of the favorite foods of the northern spotted owl, which is a threatened species in Oregon's mountains. Laws have been passed to stop trees from being cut down in the forests where this owl likes to nest. Another forest creature is the northern flying squirrel, which likes to eat lichen and plants.

A herd of elk travels through a field in northwestern Oregon. Male elk grow antlers which they sometimes use when fighting other male elk.

Bigger animals, such as elk and black-tailed deer, also live in the woods. Higher elevations in the Cascades are home to bighorn sheep, mountain goats, bobcats, coyotes, foxes, and minks.

One of Oregon's most well-known creatures, however, is the slug. Different types of slugs can be found throughout the country, but certain types are common in Oregon. The banana slug is a large slug that can be found in Oregon's damp soils. It is often yellow and very slimy. Some banana slugs can grow to be more than 6 inches long. Slugs like to eat plants and flowers, which is often a problem for many gardeners.

Some scientists believe that slugs eat more plant material in Oregon's forests than the state's large herds of elk.

The list of birds that make their homes in Oregon is very long. It includes black birds, blue birds, ducks, geese, eagles, egrets, finches, flickers, nutcrackers, and owls. Oregon is located on the migratory trail of many different kinds of birds. This means that they pass through Oregon as they travel during the different seasons. As one season changes into the next, the bird songs that Oregonians might hear change as flocks of different migrating birds come and go.

Some fish in the region are also migratory. In many of the state's waterways, there are large amounts of salmon from late summer through the fall. Trout are another type of fish that are very popular with Oregonians who like to go fishing. Because of overfishing, pollution, and other forms of human interference, wild populations of many types of fish are decreasing. In order to keep the rivers and lakes supplied, many fish farms have been established throughout the state. These farms breed and raise fish to be released into the state's waterways.

Endangered Animals in Oregon

Throughout history, many types of animals around the world have become extinct. This is supposed to be a natural process, in which a species or type of animal dies off. However, in recent times, the rate of extinction has grown faster. This is due to human interference. Settlement and pollution have destroyed habitats. The overhunting of certain animals has also caused some animal populations to decrease, allowing other animal populations to increase. When an animal population gets dangerously low, the government and other agencies label it as endangered. Laws usually protect endangered species so that they do not become extinct.

Endangered animals and fish in Oregon include the gray wolf, certain types of salmon in the Columbia and Snake Rivers, and the brown pelican. Threatened species, which are those that are almost endangered, include the bald eagle, the northern spotted owl, and the Oregon silverspot butterfly.

Nature is very important to Oregonians. That is why they work so hard to keep the environment clean, to protect all the creatures that live in the wild, and to make sure that the beautiful forests and clear waterways will be there to be enjoyed by future generations. With its variety of landscapes from rainforests to dry desert plains, Oregon remains one of the most exciting and beautiful places to live.

Though they once freely roamed through Oregon, experts believe that there are no more wild populations of gray wolves in the state.

Plants & Animals

Northern Spotted Owl

The northern spotted owl is on the threatened species list and lives in the states of Washington, Oregon, and California. The reason it is threatened is because its habitat, which is old-growth forests, is quickly disappearing due to the harvesting of the large trees that make up these forests. Oregon has the largest population of this threatened species of bird, with about 1,200 pairs.

Great Blue Heron

The Great Blue Heron lives along both saltwater shorelines and around rivers. In Oregon, you might see one of these large birds at a refuge along the Pacific shore or on the sides of one of Oregon's great rivers, such as the Rogue. Its feathers are a bluish-gray, and it has a black stripe above each eye, and very long legs.

Skunks

Skunks, easily recognized by their black coats and white stripes, are naturally very shy. But if they are threatened, they can shoot a very smelly liquid from their musk glands, hitting targets as far as 20 feet away.

Blackberries

Blackberry bushes grow wild in almost all areas of Oregon. They grow in backyards, in the median strips along major highways, and in the woods. Their brambles and leaves are very thorny, and once established in your yard, they are very hard to get rid of. But if you can tame the bushes, you will be rewarded with a very tasty fruit in August.

Pacific Giant Salamander

This is the largest salamander found in Oregon. It has a big head and muscular legs and can grow to be 13 inches long. Its has a marbled pattern skin that is tan and reddish-brown. Salamanders like cool, moist forests and tend to live underground except at night when they like to come out. The Pacific Giant Salamander is the only salamander that can make a noise—a sort of low-pitched yelp.

Chinook Salmon

Chinook salmon (sometimes called king salmon) are the largest salmon found in the Pacific Northwest. Salmon are born in freshwater streams. Once they mature, they swim into the ocean. Some salmon travel 2,000 miles away from their birthplace. After several years spent in the ocean, salmon return to mate in the same stream in which they were hatched. The Chinook salmon is Oregon's state fish.

2 From the Beginning

The First People

From about 15,000 BCE until the middle of the sixteenth century, the only people who lived in what is now called Oregon were the ancestors of present-day Native Americans. These ancestors probably came to North American from Asia, crossing a land bridge that used to connect the two continents.

The groups that chose this region as their new home soon discovered the many different kinds of food that were available. The bays, rivers, and ocean were filled with salmon, shellfish, and sea mammals. The fertile soil in the regions now know as the Willamette and Rogue valleys provided wild fruits, nuts, and nutritious roots. They also benefited from the forests in their new land. They could hunt deer, elk, sheep, and antelope. The trees from these forests supplied wood for their homes, tools, and boats. Some of these early people hunted the animals that lived in the woods. The groups that settled in the eastern section of present-day Oregon found that the natural grasslands were good places to raise horses. They also

Long before European and American settlers came to the region, Native Americans made their homes in the Pacific Northwest. White settlement eventually changed the Natives' ways of life.

Early Native Americans used spears to catch fish in the region's rivers and falls.

used the bark and timber that they found there to build their homes and boats.

Several different Native groups lived throughout the region. In the south-central section the prominent people were the Klamath-Modoc. The Paiute people lived in caves during the harsh winters in the deserts of east. In the northeastern corner the Nez Percé, one of the largest groups to lived on the Columbia Plateau, used tents for homes. The Nez Percé were known for their skills in raising and riding horses.

The Clackamas and Kalapuya people lived in the Willamette Valley. Along the Pacific Coast were the Clatsop, the Tillamook, the Siuslaw, the Umpqua, and the Coquille. Many Oregonians today are familiar with the names of these groups because these names are used to identify certain rivers and forests in the state. Unfortunately, there is not very much information about many of these first people, although they lived in the region for thousands of years.

The First Europeans

It was not until the middle of the sixteenth century that white Europeans saw the land that would one day be called Oregon. Some of the first Europeans to come close to these shores were Spanish explorers who were looking for gold. They had heard rumors that there were secret cities filled with gold in North America. They sailed their ships northward from Mexico, looking for a river that would allow them to sail deeper into the North American continent. But when these earliest ships reached the area around present-day Oregon, heavy storms kept them from getting any closer than the Pacific shoreline.

Once the rumors of gold spread, many European countries became interested in the Pacific Northwest. Each country sent ships up and down the shore, looking for rivers that would allow them to travel across North America. Russia and England set up fur-trading posts in the areas we now know as Alaska and Canada. Spain built outposts in the region that includes California. Each country, at one time or another, claimed that the land of the Pacific Northwest was theirs. In 1775, Bruno de Hezeta claimed the land for Spain because he believed he was the first European who actually stood on the land.

Several years later, in 1792, an American explorer named Robert Gray successfully guided his ship into a wild and dangerous river, which he named after his ship, the *Columbia Rediviva*. Robert Gray became known as the first white person

Historians believe that the Columbia River was named after Robert Gray's ship, the Columbia Rediviva.

to sail up the Columbia River. He claimed the land, which became known as the Oregon Country, for the United States.

The Lewis and Clark Expedition

In 1803, under President Jefferson's leadership, the United States bought an extremely large area of land, called the Louisiana Purchase. With this land, the country doubled in size. But President Jefferson wanted the country to extend from the Atlantic to the Pacific Oceans. To make part of that dream come true, he organized a group of explorers called the Corps of Discovery. President Jefferson wanted the Corps to study the western land, to make maps of the area, to befriend the Native people, all in the hopes that one day the United States could claim all of the territory. The Corps would travel from the Missouri River to the furthest point west in search of a waterway that would allow ships to travel across the entire continent. He appointed Meriwether Lewis to lead the group. Lewis asked William Clark to assist him, beginning the adventures of the Lewis and Clark expedition.

Lewis and Clark began their trip in 1804. It would prove to be a very difficult but very important journey. Due to Lewis and Clark's success, a path was forged that many settlers would soon follow. Although Lewis and Clark did not find a Northwest Passage for boats to use to travel across the United States, the reports about their adventures inspired thousands of other people to move west.

The Oregon Trail

By the 1840s, people were pouring into Oregon Country through a pathway known as the Oregon Trail. Thousands of wagon trains made the difficult journey, which for many people began in Independence, Missouri, and ended just south of Portland in a small town called Oregon City. The trip was over 2,000 miles long and often took four to five months to complete. The trail crossed three mountain ranges: the Rocky Mountains, the Blue Mountains, and the Cascades. Most people traveled in large covered wagons, called prairie schooners, which were usually pulled by a team of oxen.

Many people died during the journey, but this did not stop wagon trains. People from all over the world had caught the "Oregon Fever," and they were anxious to find what they hoped would be a new and wonderful life once they reached Willamette Valley.

Statehood

People came to the Oregon Country for many different reasons. Some came for the fur trade and trapped animals, such as beavers, and sold the skins. Other people came as missionaries, hoping to persuade Native Americans to practice Christianity. In order to encourage new settlers to the area, a law called the Oregon Land Law was passed in 1850. This law gave more than 300 acres of free land to anyone who promised to plant crops on it. The idea of free land brought a new wave of people to Oregon Country. Then in 1851, gold was discovered in southern Oregon, and like California before it, Oregon experienced a gold rush.

In 1845, Francis Pettygrove was responsible for naming Oregon's largest city. Mr. Pettygrove had lived in Portland, Maine. He liked the name of his hometown so much that he decided to give his new Oregon city the same name.

Settlers from the Midwest and the East Coast traveled across plains, forests, and mountains to make new lives in the region.

Making a Pinwheel

Children on wagon trains going to Oregon often made their own games and toys. One simple toy was the pinwheel. Many boys and girls made pinwheels and attached them to the wagons to watch the spinning colors as the wagon moved or as the wind blew.

What You Need

1 sheet of stiff paper (a manila file folder, oak
   tag, or thick construction paper)
Ruler
Pencil
Crayons or markers
Scissors
1 pin
Long unsharpened pencil with an eraser

Use the ruler and pencil to draw a 6-inch square on the paper. Cut out the square. Draw diagonal lines from each corner, but stop each line 1 inch from the center of the square.

Draw a big dot in the center of the square.

Using the crayons or markers, draw small circles or stars in part of each of the corners. (Only color the corners shown in the illustration here.)

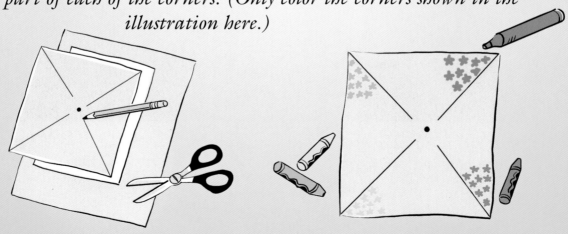

Use the scissors to cut a straight line from each corner. You should cut along the diagonal lines you drew earlier. Stop cutting about 1 inch from the center.

With the decorated side of the paper facing away from you, bend each decorated corner toward you so that all four decorated points meet at the center. Overlap the tips a little bit so the pin will go through all four folded corners.

Place the unsharpened pencil behind the paper, with the eraser against the center. Push the pin through the four tips, then through the center. The sharp end of the pin should stick into the pencil's eraser. Be careful when you push the pin through the paper—you do not want to get pricked.

Blow on the pinwheel or put it outside in the wind and watch the colors spin. You can experiment with different designs and colors to see what neat patterns the spinning colors make.

Oregon City was founded along the Willamette River at the end of the Oregon Trail. It served as the Oregon Territory's first capital.

With all these trappers, missionaries, settlers, and gold miners rushing into the Oregon Country, the Native American population began to suffer. In 1805, it was estimated that more than 40,000 Native Americans lived in the Oregon Territory. But their numbers were decreasing. The trappers were killing animals that the Native Americans had once relied on for food. The settlers were claiming land that had once belonged to the Native population. The miners polluted the waters when they dug for gold. White people also brought diseases with them, such as measles, which killed many of the Native American children. Tensions grew between the Natives and the white people, and several wars broke out. Not all of the Native groups got along with one another, so the Native people had a hard time banding together to drive out the new settlers. But the Natives still fought the newcomers to protect and reclaim their land.

The new Oregonians pleaded with government officials in Washington, D.C., to give them more protection from the Native Americans. One way for the white Oregonians to protect themselves was to ask the government to recognize their territory as an official state. In 1857, a statewide convention was called to create a state constitution. Two years later on Februay 14, 1859, President James Buchanan made Oregon the thirty-third state.

Becoming a state did not end all the difficulties between the white settlers and the Native Americans. However, once Oregon became a state, its citizens could request help from the United States Army. The government also created reservations and forced Native Americans to leave their homes and live on the reservations. The army also made sure that the Native Americans obeyed the white people's laws. The Native population began to decrease in size, while the white population continued to grow. By the end of the 1800s, the Native population in the region dropped to less than 10,000.

As American settlements grew, the settlers and the Native Americans were drawn into bloody battles.

When the transcontinental railroad line reached Oregon in the 1880s, travel to the new state became much easier, and the number of people living in the state grew rapidly. Between 1900 and 1910, for instance, Portland's population grew from 90,000 to 200,000. Some of the people who arrived during this time were not as interested in being farmers or ranchers as the people who had come before them. Many of these new people were used to living cities, so they developed Oregon's cities, building new stores and other types of businesses.

The railroad also provided a way of transporting goods from Oregon to other parts of the nation. Wheat and lumber grown in Oregon could be shipped back East. This meant that

Railroads that crossed the Cascade Mountains helped to increase business and trade to and from the growing state.

more people could buy these products, and Oregon's economy began to grow.

Around the turn of the twentieth century, people other than those of European descent began to move to Oregon. Immigrants from Asia, particularly from Japan and China, made Oregon their home. By 1900, Portland had the second largest "Chinatown" in the United States. The African-American community also increased in population during this time. Despite the fact that the early settlers of Oregon were not very tolerant of people who were not white, a racially mixed population in Oregon continued to expand. Factories were built in Oregon's cities, creating jobs for many residents.

Loggers pause beside a giant Douglas fir around 1918. Oregon's dense forests provided countless trees for the state's growing lumber industry.

Hard times hit Oregon—and the rest of the nation—with the Great Depression. Starting in 1929, this was a period of time when the country's economy was very bad. Banks and businesses closed and people lost their jobs and their homes. The federal government established work programs to help the unemployed while also rebuilding the country. Workers were hired to do things such as

During the Great Depression, people from across the country traveled to Oregon in search of jobs. Many men and women worked in the states farms and forests.

constructing roads, cutting down forests, and building dams. In the 1930s dams, such as the Bonneville Dam on the Columbia River, were built in Oregon. These dams helped to create electric power and also provide water for farms.

The United States fought in World War II starting in 1941. The war helped improve the economy. Factories needed workers to make supplies for the war effort. Oregon farms also supplied the troops with food.

Unfortunately, after World War II, especially during the 1950s and 1960s, everything in Oregon seemed to slow down. Fewer people were moving into the state, and the state's economy became one of the worst in the entire nation. It was also during this time that Oregonians began to look around their state and notice that some of their industries also caused great environmental damage. Factories had turned the Willamette River into a sewer, contaminating the river with their waste. The Willamette was declared the most polluted river in the Pacific Northwest and one of the most polluted waterways in the United States. In other places, mountainsides were completely stripped of trees. This caused dangerous mudslides that clogged rivers and damaged homes. So Oregonians became determined to make their state healthy again.

The Smallest City Park in the World can be found in Salem, where Judge William Waldo, in 1936, planted a Sierra Redwood on the northwest corner of the intersection of Union Street and Summer Street. The park is only 12 feet by 20 feet wide (about the size of a small living room) and is called Waldo Park.

By the end of the 1960s, Oregonians voted for antipollution laws that helped clean up their environment. By the 1970s, Oregon became the state with the most laws that had been created to protect natural resources.

Oregon Today

Oregon is a state that is rich in natural beauty. Its wide range of natural resources, however, needs to be taken care of. Today, the people of Oregon know that they

Throughout the state's history, cities like Portland have become important centers of business and culture.

cannot over-fish their rivers or the fish will become endangered. They know that if they clear-cut all their forests, they will eventually run out of trees and damage the state's streams and rivers because of mudslides. The conservation of natural resources is sometimes a very difficult thing to do. But Oregonians are committed to keeping it healthy and clean. This not only makes Oregon a great place to live, it also attracts people from other states who enjoy visiting Oregon's beaches, mountains, and deserts. The money that tourists spend helps to create jobs. And the taxes that tourists pay help to improve services that Oregonians need.

Although Oregon is changing, in many ways it also remains the same. Just like in the pioneer days, people from all over the nation still hear that Oregon is a great place to live. The air quality is good. The temperatures are mild. And the natural environment offers many exciting outdoor adventures. Although traveling to Oregon is not as hard as it used to be hundreds of years ago, when people come to the state they still find a land of green rolling hills and a great place to establish a new home. In other words, people who come to Oregon can still feel like they have discovered a new paradise.

Oregonians have learned from past mistakes, and for years have been working on treasuring and protecting the land they call home.

Important Dates

12,000 BCE The first Native people of Oregon begin to move from Asia by crossing the land bridge across the Bering Strait.

1543 CE Spanish navigator, Bartolome Ferrelo, sailing up the coast from Mexico, becomes the first white person to sight the Oregon coast.

1775 Bruno de Hezeta claims he is the first white person to set food on land around the Columbia River and claims the land for Spain.

1792 Robert Gray successfully guides his boat, the *Columbia Rediviva*, into the river that he will later name in honor of his ship.

1843 Pioneers from all over the states begin a major immigration to Oregon along the Oregon Trail.

1844 Slavery is declared illegal in Oregon.

1845 Francis Pettygrove names the new city on the Columbia River after his hometown of Portland, Maine.

William Clark

1846 Eugene Skinner establishes the city of Eugene in the Willamette Valley.

1848 The U.S. Congress officially recognizes Oregon as a territory.

1851 Gold is discovered in eastern and southern Oregon.

1853 Oregon Territory is separated from Washington.

1859 On February 14, Oregon becomes the thirty-third state.

1877 Chief Joseph tries to lead his people, the Nez Percé, from Oregon to Canada to get away from the U.S. Army.

1883 The transcontinental railroad reaches Portland.

1932 Oregon's first dam, the Owyhee Dam, is built on the Owyhee River.

1951 Oregon passes the country's first air-pollution laws.

1980 Mount St. Helens erupts and drops volcanic ash over much of the state.

1984 Margaret Carter is the first African-American woman elected to the Oregon House of Representatives.

Mount St. Helens erupting

1990 Oregonians elect their first female governor, Barbara Roberts.

1998 The Willamette River is proclaimed one of the nation's fourteen American Heritage Rivers for its historical, cultural, and environmental significance.

2001 The Chinook Indian Tribe is formally recognized by the U.S. government.

3 The People

Native Americans

Not a lot is known about the earliest people who lived on the land that is now Oregon. But many assume that the rich food sources that were found along the Pacific Coast helped to feed Oregon's first inhabitants. They probably existed on a diet that included clams, salmon, oysters, seals, and whales. Many of these early people probably traveled by water, up and down the ocean coast as well as into the interior of the land, using the many rivers and creeks. The fertile valleys of Willamette, Rogue, and Cowlitz provided fruits and nuts.

Although the beliefs of the many different groups varied, people who have studied their history think that the original settlers of the region were very aware of protecting the environment. They lived in this area for several thousands of years with little sign of pollution or of endangering the wildlife. "Over time," writes Gordon B. Dodds in his book *The American Northwest,* "the first inhabitants worked out a system of

A young Oregonian poses for a picture near his home on the Warm Springs Indian Reservation near Madras. Today, Native Americans make up only a very small portion of the state's population.

A Native American resident pulls a net used for fishing from the Deschutes River. Many of the state's Natives try to practice the traditional ways of their ancestors.

land management that enabled them both to use and to conserve natural resources."

A little more is known about some of the later people who lived in this area. One of those groups was the Klamath-Modoc, who lived in the southernmost part of the area. They moved according to the season. In the winter, they lived inside dwellings they built. In other seasons, they lived out in the open and followed the trails of animals, which provided them with food. Some of the food they ate were the eggs of swans, ducks, and other birds that lived on upper Klamath Lake. They also used spears and nets to catch fish. Before winter brought snow, the men hunted bigger animals, such as deer, antelope, and sheep.

Another group was the Paiute, who lived on the easternmost borders of Oregon, a harsh land that was dry and very hot in the summer and very cold in the winter. The Paiute tended to live in caves because they were continually moving in search of food. The main part of their diet was rabbit and antelope.

There are many stories about the Nez Percé people who lived north of the Paiute in northeastern Oregon. Their most famous leader was Chief Joseph who tried to save his people from being forced to live on a reservation. Chief Joseph attempted to lead his people to Canada to escape the United States Army. Many times, Chief Joseph outsmarted the army, but in the end, he and his people finally surrendered because many members had died from the cold weather and lack of food. In a speech upon his surrender, Chief Joseph said: "Hear me, my chiefs. I am tired; my heart is sick and sad. From where the sun now stands I will fight no more forever."

The name Nez Percé (which means "pierced nose") comes from the French traders who named this group for the rings the people wore in their noses.

Other groups included the Clatsops, Clackamas, Puyallup, Nisqually, Tillamook, Siuslaw, and the Umpqua. Many of these Native American groups were completely wiped out by diseases the Europeans brought with them.

The Chinook lived along the rivers and the ocean shoreline. They were one of the largest groups and some of the most successful traders. The Chinook's ability to trade made them one of the richest Native groups in all of North America. They also developed a special language that helped them speak to European traders, whether the traders came from French- or English-speaking countries. This language was called Chinook Jargon and was made up of French, English, and several different Native words.

Many Native Americans honor their culture and traditions by taking part in powwows and festivals.

Today Oregon is home to several Native American reservations. The Confederated Tribes of the Umatilla Reservation in northeastern Oregon includes members of the Cayuse, the Umatilla, and the Walla Walla People. The Klamath people live in south-central Oregon. This includes the Klamaths, the Modocs, and the Yahooskin. And on the eastern slopes of the Cascades, the Confederated Tribes of Warm Springs make their homes. This is where the Warm Springs tribe, the Wasco and the Paiute people share a reservation. In the west, you will find the Confederate Tribes of Grand Ronde, which has the largest population of all the Native American reservations in Oregon.

However, not all Native Americans live on reservations. There were 45,211 Native Americans listed on the 2000 Census. Of this number, almost 90 percent of Native Americans live in cities, not on reservations. In recent years, Native American groups have appealed to the government to abide by old treaties that have, for a long time, been ignored. These treaties were supposed to grant the Natives certain righs and property. In the past, in order to bring the Native American population into the main culture of the United States, many Native groups were officially terminated by the state government. The government thought this would help the Native population. However, in many cases it did not. So today, Oregon officials are working very hard to reestablish traditional Native groups and to make new laws that will protect Native American rights.

Mountain Men, Fur Trappers, and Missionaries

The first white people to see Oregon Country were the Spanish, who sailed along Oregon's coast in 1543. However,

Robert Gray, an American, was the first to sail inland using the Columbia River. Fur traders and fur trappers, sometimes referred to as mountain men, explored the area, but none of established a community in Oregon. It was not until 1811 that a permanent settlement was built at the mouth of the Columbia River. That was when John Jacob Astor, an American fur trader, set up a post in what would soon become the small town of Astoria.

The missionaries came next. They were religious people who traveled to the West to teach Native Americans about Christianity. It is believed that the missionaries actually came to Oregon based on misinformation. In 1831, some Nez Perce people traveled east to St. Louis, Missouri, looking for members of the Lewis and Clark Expedition. They were in search of better tools and weapons, which they had seen members of the Expedition use. Because they did not speak English, the Nez Perce people were misunderstood. Rumors spread that the Nez Perce people were looking for a new religion. Once the missionaries heard these rumors, many of them made plans to travel West.

The first group of missionaries were lead by Jason Lee, who, in 1834, set up a permanent settlement in Willamette Valley, outside of present-day Salem. The most famous of the missionaries, however, were Marcus and Narcissa Whitman, who actually built their mission in Walla Walla, Washington. Their work, however, included Oregon's Nez Percé. The Whitmans not only preached Christian beliefs to Native Americans, they also helped many travelers on the Oregon Trail. The Whitmans helped save many lives by providing pioneers with medicine and food. Unfortunately, a group of Native Americans blamed the Whitmans for an outbreak of measles, and the increasing numbers of settlers. Cayuse warriors—angered by these circumstances—killed the Whitmans and other missionaries.

Cultural Make-up

During the late nineteenth and early twentieth centuries, people from all over the world came to Oregon. Many groups came to the new state with special skills, which helped them find jobs their new homeland. For instance, many Greek people had special talents that helped them work on the railroads. Many Swedish people worked in lumber mills. Norwegians and people from Finland

Over the years, people from around the country have made Oregon their home.

knew a lot about fishing, while people from Denmark were good dairy farmers. There were also a lot of Irish people and people from Mexico who were skilled in mining. Many Italian immigrants were very good farmers.

Junction City, located outside of Eugene, was settled by people from Denmark, Finland, Norway, and Sweden. To celebrates their Scandinavian heritage, the people of Junction City transform their downtown into an authentic old-world village every summer. They dress up in authentic costumes, dance to traditional music, and cook traditional food.

Famous Oregonians

Chief Joseph: Native American Leader

Chief Joseph was born in northeastern Oregon. His given name was Hin-mah-too-yah-lat-kekt, which means, "Thunder Rolling Down the Mountain." He became chief of the Nez Percé as white people moved onto the area, and demanded that the Nez Percé give up their land. At first the government gave in and allowed the Nez Percé people to stay on their land, but later this ruling was changed. Chief Joseph tried to lead his people to safety. In the end, however, he and his people were taken to Oklahoma and eventually relocated on small reservations in Washington and Idaho.

Beverly Cleary: Author

Cleary was born in McMinnville, Oregon, in 1916. She is the writer of many famous and award-winning books. Her most famous characters are Ramona Quimby and Henry Huggins, and she has written several books about them. There is even a place in Portland, Oregon, called the Beverly Cleary Sculpture Garden that contains bronze statues of her two most famous characters.

Matt Groening: Cartoonist

Groening, the creator of the television show, The Simpsons, *was born in Portland. Matt's father, whose name is Homer, was a cartoonist and encouraged Matt to draw. In 1986, Groening created* The Simpsons, *which has become the longest-running animated series on television.*

Steve Prefontaine: Athlete

Prefontaine was raised in Coos Bay, where he set track records at Marshfield High School. Later, he attended the University of Oregon, where he became the first athlete to win four consecutive NCAA titles in the 5,000 meters. Before he died at the age of twenty-four, Steve held the American record in every event from 2,000 to 10,000 meters. Crowds at Haywood field loved him for his good sportsmanship and pleasant personality. He never lost an event at the University of Oregon field.

Ann Curry: Journalist

Curry grew up in in Ashland, Oregon, and graduated with a degree in journalism from the University of Oregon. She began her career as a television reporter at a Medford station and later went to work at another station in Portland. She has won numerous prizes for her television reporting, including two Emmy Awards. Recently she has worked as the news anchor for NBC News' Today Show and is often seen on the program Dateline.

Linus Pauling: Scientist

Pauling was born in Portland and lived for a while in Condon, where his father ran a drug store. He attended Washington High School in Portland and received his bachelor's degree from Oregon State College, where he studied chemistry. He was awarded the Nobel Prize in chemistry in 1954. Later in life, he became an activist against war and was awarded the Nobel Peace Prize in 1962.

Japanese-American residents came to the region to find work. These men are traveling together to work on a farm.

People from China came to Oregon to get away from political problems and poverty in their homeland. Many Chinese people found jobs in Oregon's mines and in fish-packing industries along the Columbia River. It was also through the hard labor and courage of many Chinese men that Oregon's railroad lines were completed.

With their skills in boat building and navigation, a small population of Hawaiians moved successfully into the fur-trading businesses. Many worked as sailors, transporting furs by boat.

The first African American came to Oregon on Robert Gray's ship. Marcus Lopius was Gray's cabin boy. Unfortunately, he was killed by a group of Tillamook warriors when he went ashore to survey the land. Another legendary African American was Moses Harris, a fur trapper, who later became a guide for people traveling the Oregon Trail. There were not many

African Americans make up the state's largest minority population.

African Americans living in Oregon before it became a state. Yet some white people were concerned that black people and Native Americans might join forces and start a rebellion. So although Oregonians declared their homeland an anti-slavery state in 1857 when they wrote Oregon's constitution, they also included a rule that prohibited African Americans from living in the state. This remained in the constitution until 1929, when a majority of Oregonians voted against it.

Today, people of many different ethnic backgrounds live in Oregon, though the population remains mostly white. According to the 2000 Census figures, only 1 percent are Native American, 2 percent are African Americans, and 3 percent are Asian

Throughout Oregon's history, many families from different backgrounds have made this state their home.

American. The Hispanic population is the fastest growing minority group in the state, and it makes up only 8 percent of the total population. Although relatively small numbers of Asian Americans, Mexican Americans, Native Americans, and African Americans live in the state, Oregonians celebrate ethnic diversity through many exciting celebrations.

Portland remains Oregon's largest city with 538,544 people. Eugene is the second-largest, with 142,185. Other cities with large populations include Salem, Gresham, and Beaverton.

Oregonians enjoy their state's natural beauty.

Calendar of Events

Oregon Asian Celebration

In February, Eugene presents this celebration every year at the Lane County Fairgrounds. Two days of festivities include demonstrations of martial arts, exhibitions of ink paintings, bonsai, and other Asian arts, as well as dance performances and food.

Oregon Scottish Heritage Festival

In April, Salem features an all-day celebration at the Held at the Linn County Fairgrounds. The festival provides a taste of Scotland through music, entertainment, and food.

Fiesta Latina-Cinco de Mayo

At this festival, held in May in Eugene, you can celebrate Latino culture with music and fun. Join the dancing, enjoy the food, and learn about the arts and crafts of Latin America during this weekend party.

Old-Time Fiddlers' Contest

Wallowa sponsors its Old-Time Fiddlers' Contest each June to preserve and encourage the art of traditional old-time fiddling, just like Oregon's settlers used to play. The contest is open to fiddlers of all ages.

The Portland skyline

The Annual Celtic Festival

This is held each August in Bend. Bagpipes, dances, children's games, food, and fun are all available. Costumed eighteenth-century Royal Navy marines reenact battle scenes similar to those of the War of Independence.

Homowo Festival

This celebration, held in August, is the largest African festival of music, dance, arts, children's activities, and food presented in the Pacific Northwest. It is held in Portland each year.

Kite Festival

In September the wind blows just right at Lincoln City, in time for this festival. Special activities include Kiteboarding, Kanine Kiting, Kite Ballet, and Rokkaku Kite Battles.

Greek Festival in Portland

Portland's Greek community sponsors a festival in October. If you are curious about Greek culture, food, and music, this is a good event to attend.

Portland's ZooLights

From November to December, take a ride through the park on a train decorated with thousands of lights. Listen to a hundred different musical groups sing traditional and seasonal songs. There is also holiday treats to eat and animal characters to entertain you.

A kite festival

4 How It Works

At the beginning of Oregon's history, there was more than one set of laws by which people who lived in the area tried to keep law and order. Native American groups were ruled by tribal laws. French Canadians and British fur-trappers followed the laws of their home countries. However, new settlers, missionaries, and sailors, who lived in the Oregon Territory, had no laws to protect them. This was because Oregon was not yet a state. So in 1843, a group of 102 settlers came together and selected a committee to write a constitution. The constitution was called the Organic Act and was written in Oregon City on July 5. On this day, the Provisional Government of Oregon was born.

The Provisional Government of Oregon was based on the same form as the United States government. It had a legislature and a judicial system. However, instead of using a governor to head the executive branch, a committee of three people shared this role. This did not prove to be very successful, though, so in 1845, George Abernethy became the first governor of Oregon Country. In 1857, the present-day constitution was

This pioneer statue is 23 feet tall and sits atop the state Capitol. It represents the spirit of the state's settlers.

adopted. Then in 1859, "Honest John" Whiteaker became the first elected governor of Oregon, which had become an official state.

Oregon's Modern Government

The basic form of Oregon's state government has not changed much over the years. There is an executive branch, a legislative branch, and a judicial branch. These three branches work together to make laws and make sure the laws are obeyed and that they benefit the state.

Barbara Roberts was the first woman to be elected as the governor of Oregon.

Oregon also has local governments that serve the cities and counties. Oregon's cities use a form of home rule, which means each city has the right to choose its own form of government. The people of Portland use a mayor and four commissioners to guide their city. In other cities, a city manager and a council take care of government affairs. A third kind of government is used in the smaller cities. They use a mayor and a city council. Oregon's thirty-six counties also have a form of government. In each county, elected members work together on a board of commissioners.

How a Bill Becomes a Law

All of Oregon's laws begin with someone coming up with an idea. This idea can come from just about anyone: an ordinary citizen, a group of citizens, a senator, a representative, or a judge, just to name a few. Some of the ideas that have become bills in the past have created new laws, removed old laws, or asked for money for special projects. In order for a bill to become a law, it must go through many different steps.

First the idea is given to either a senator or a representative, who must sponsor, or accept, it. If the bill is sponsored by a senator, then it is first presented to the full senate. If it is sponsored by a representative, then it first goes to the house of representatives.

Branches of Government

Executive The governor of Oregon serves as the head of the executive branch. Serving under the governor is the attorney general, the labor commissioner, the secretary of state, the superintendent of public instruction, and the state treasurer. The governor is elected to a four-year term.

Legislative This branch of government is made up of the state senate and the state house of representatives. There are thirty senators and sixty representatives. Senators serve four-year terms and can serve no more than two terms. Representatives serve two-year terms.

Judicial The Supreme Court is the highest court in the state. There are seven Supreme Court justices. Ten judges serve in the next highest court, the court of appeals. The circuit courts are where most trials are held. Eighty-seven judges serve the circuit courts. Each judge, no matter in which court they serve, is elected to a six-year term.

Next, the bill is given to the lawyers in the Legislative Counsels office, where it is written in correct legal language. A special number is assigned to the bill by the chief clerk of the house or senate. Before it returns to the senate or the house, it is printed and read one more time by the lawyers.

The bill is then returned to either the senate, or the house, for its first official reading. After the senators or the representatives have all heard it, the bill is sent to a committee. The members of the committee consider the bill and present it to the public to get their reactions. After final consideration, the bill is returned to where it started, either to the senate or to the house, and it is read again. Committee members might have changed the bill when they were considering it, so everyone must be brought up to date on those amendments, or changes. The bill is read again for the third time, and this time the members of the senate or house vote on it. In order to pass, the bill must receive at least thirty-one votes in the house and sixteen votes in the senate.

Unlike other state capitols, the Oregon State Capitol does not have a rounded dome.

After the bill has passed in both the house and the senate, it is signed by the speaker of the house or the senate president, and the chief clerk of the house or the secretary of the senate. Then it is sent to the governor. If the governor signs it, the bill becomes law. The governor also has the power to veto, or vote against, the bill. If this happens, the senate and the house members can vote for it again. If the member of the senate and the house vote in favor of the bill, with two-thirds of the members present, then they can override the governor's veto.

There is a Web site that is filled with information about Oregon's government. Here you can find the name of Oregon's senators and representatives, history about the state, biographies of famous Oregonians, and other interesting facts. There is a special section for students, too. Keep up with current events in the state, read about initiatives, as well as find many links to other interesting Web sites at this address: http://bluebook.state.or.us/

One of the most interesting things about Oregon's government is what is called Oregon's initiatives. Initiatives allow citizens to be more active in making laws and changing the constitution. Citizens come up with a new idea, gather a number of signatures, and the initiative is then printed on the ballots. Then everyone in the state can vote either for or against it.

5 Making a Living

Oregon's economy has come a long way from the pioneer days when fur trading was the best way to earn a living. Although fur trapping is no longer a business in Oregon, three things that provided pioneers with a good life still bring a lot of money to the state today. These three things are Oregon's thick forests, its fertile soils, and its abundant seafood.

Forest products

Throughout much of the nineteenth century and most of the twentieth century, Oregon's forests provided lumber for the entire nation. New houses all over the United States were often built with Oregon lumber. Oregon also leads the nation in the production of Christmas trees, which are grown specifically to be cut down in the winter for the holidays. Oregonians are not the only ones who enjoy these trees. Oregon's Christmas trees are shipped to every state. Other things made of wood include paper and cardboard, the products of another big business in the state. In 1950, the manufacturing of lumber and wood

John Day Fossil Beds National Monument provides visitors with amazing views of land features created by nature over time.

The lumber industry is still an important part of Oregon's economy.

products provided jobs to almost 50 percent of Oregon's population. By 2001, that number had fallen to only 21 percent. But Oregon's lumber industry is still important to the state.

Agriculture

Agriculture is big business in Oregon. In 2002, there were 41,000 working farms. Each farm had an average of 420 acres, and most were run by families, not big corporations.

This vineyard is located in the Willamette Valley.

Most farms are located in Marion, Clackamas, Washington, Umatilla, and Yamhill counties.

Other major crops that are grown in Oregon's fertile soils include hazelnuts, peppermint, raspberries, blackberries, sweet cherries, pears, cauliflower, and onions, just to name a few. Wheat is another very important product.

One of Oregon's most popular exports—products that are shipped out of the state—is frozen French fries.

Oregon farmers are some of the most efficient farmers in the world. This means that they grow large crops without wasting a lot of money or land. It has been estimated that each farmer produces enough food to feed 130 people. Because of Oregon's successful farmers, most Oregonians do not have to worry about growing their own food.

Oregon also raises a lot of cows. In 2001, Oregon made nearly $500 million in the sale of beef. The state also made $223 million in the sale of milk. Beef and milk are listed as two of the top five things produced in the state. Grass seed, hay, and greenhouse and nursery products were the other three.

Wildlife

Another major industry in Oregon is based on the abundant wildlife in the state. In particular, many businesses make a lot of money off of fish. Some of

Livestock is an important part of Oregon's agricultural industry.

Recipe for Blackberry and Hazelnut Cookie Bars

Ingredients:

For the bottom crust

1/2 cup butter
1 tablespoons sugar
1-1/2 cups flour

For the middle filling

5 cups fresh blackberries (you can use
    frozen blackberries)
3/4 cup flour
1-3/4 cup sugar

For the final topping

1/2 cup brown sugar
1/3 cup butter
1/2 cup flour

1/2 cup raw oatmeal (old fashioned kind, not instant)
1 teaspoon cinnamon
1/2 cup chopped hazelnuts

Mix together the three ingredients for the crust until everything is nicely blended. Then press the crust into the bottom of a lightly greased 9 inch by 13 inch baking pan.

For the filling, first wash the blackberries and mix them with a spoon. Combine the berries with the flour and sugar. Then pour the filling onto the top of the crust and spread it around.

In a bowl, mix together the ingredients for the topping. The topping will be crumbly. Sprinkle it on top of the blackberry filling so the top is all covered.

Have an adult help you place the pan into a preheated oven (350 degrees) for one hour. Let it cool for about 15 minutes before you cut it into squares. Then enjoy them with some cool milk or some hot chocolate!

these businesses include canneries, fish and tackle supply stores, restaurants, and commercial fishing boats. There are more than 62,000 miles of fishing streams, 1,600 lakes and reservoirs, and, of course, the long Pacific shoreline in Oregon. The fish in these bodies of water not only provide food for Oregonians and people all over the world, they also provide fun for people who like to fish as a sport. Over 700,000 people apply for fishing licenses each year in Oregon. Salmon and trout are the most popular fish to catch.

People also come to Oregon to hunt. Hunters spend about $600 million in Oregon each year. The animals that are hunted include deer, elk, pronghorn antelope, and bighorn sheep. Cougar and bear, as well as water fowl such as ducks and geese are also hunted.

Minerals and Metals

Oregon's supply of natural gas and various types of minerals is a new and growing industry. The sale of sand and gravel, cement and lime, crushed rock and other building materials, and clay and pumice is yet another way Oregonians make a living. Oregon

A cement plant uses gravel, minerals, and other material taken from Oregon land.

also has a supply of gold and gemstones, such as agates, obsidian, and sunstones. Aluminum and steel and also made in Oregon.

Technology

Another new type of business that has recently supplied money and jobs for Oregonians is the technology industry. These businesses manufacture computer software, microcomputer chips, and other computer-based products. Hewlett-Packard, a company that manufactures computers and printers moved some operations to Oregon in 1975. Intel came to Oregon a year later. A division of Symantec—which makes computer programs and provides other computer-related services—has offices in Eugene.

Service and Tourism

The service industry produces the most money in Oregon. Included under services are businesses such as insurance companies, department stores, health care companies, law firms, real estate businesses, banks, schools, and hospitals. Transportation is also included under services. The service industry also includes businesses such as trucking companies, television stations, and telephone companies.

Tourism is a vital part of Oregon's economy. Visitors to the state spend millions of dollars every year.

Products & Resources

Wheat

Wheat is Oregon's most valuable food crop. Most of it grows in the north-central part of the state. In 1980, Oregon farmers grew 77 million bushels of wheat, a record production.

Christmas Trees

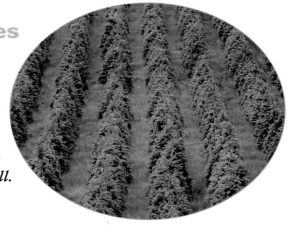

Oregon is the biggest producer of Christmas trees, selling almost ten million of them each year. Some of the most popular types of Christmas trees are the scotch pine and the Douglas and Noble firs. It takes six to ten years for these trees to grow big enough to sell.

Lighthouses

The seacoast is one of Oregon's favorite tourist attractions. One thing you might enjoy on a trip to the coast is visiting some of the historic lighthouses located there. One of the most beautiful is the old lighthouse at Heceta Head, which was built in 1894. The light at Heceta Head is one of the strongest on the coast. It shines twenty-one miles out to sea to warn ships of the rocky shoreline.

Seafood

The seafood harvested from the Pacific Coast is important to the state's economy. Oregonians are very protective of their salmon and other fish. Each year, school children stamp the silhouette of a fish near street drainage pipes, reminding everyone in their neighborhood not to dump toxic wastes into the sewers. The sewers flow into the state's waterways, and seafood can be harmed by the dumped waste.

Hazelnuts

With Oregon's fertile soil, rain, and sun, the state provides the perfect environment in which to grow hazelnuts. Around 99 percent of the hazelnut crop in the United States is grown in Willamette Valley. The first hazelnut tree in Oregon was planted in 1858. One amazing fact about the hazelnut is that these trees can produce nuts for over 80 years.

Tourism

There are thirteen national forests located in Oregon. Most of them are located in the mountains and along the rivers. Residents and tourists enjoy many outdoor activities in these parks, including backpacking, fishing, kayaking, skiing, mountain biking, as well as bird and wildlife watching.

Tourism is also included in the service industry. Oregon's tourism industry—which includes people who own hotels and restaurants, as well as tourist attractions like aquariums, museums, casinos, and state parks—made more than six billion dollars in 2001. Tourism is one of Oregon's top five industries. When tourists come to the state they not only spend money, they also provide jobs, because someone has to serve them. Waiters at restaurants benefit from tourists, as well as people who own gas stations and other businesses.

Oregon, with its sandy beaches on the Pacific Coast, its tall, snow-capped mountains in the interior, and its high deserts along the eastern border, is often considered a natural wonderland in the United States. The powerful natural surroundings draw Oregonians outside, rain or shine, and make them feel happy and proud to be living in a place where the trees grow tall, the rivers run clear, and many people greet one another with welcoming smiles. With its rich history and bright future, the Beaver State is a great place to see.

Oregon has the only state flag that has two different designs, one on the front and one on the back. The flag is navy blue with gold lettering and designs. On the front are the words, "State of Oregon," which sit atop a gold shield. Below the shield is the number, "1859," the year Oregon was admitted as a state. The shield contains the state seal. On the reverse side of the flag is a golden image of the beaver, referring to one of Oregon's nicknames, the Beaver State.

Around the top of the outer circle are the words, "State of Oregon." Around the bottom is the year, "1859," Oregon's year of statehood. Above the inner circle is a bald eagle with its wings spread wide. The eagle is sitting on top of a shield. In this shield is a picture of the sun setting over the Pacific Ocean, the mountains, and forests, representing the natural resources of Oregon. There is also a covered wagon, standing for the pioneers who came to Oregon. A plow, a sheaf of wheat, and a pickax stand for the early agriculture and mining industries. There are two ships representing the victory of the United States over Britain in controlling the Oregon territory. Around the bottom of the inner circle are thirty-three stars, representing Oregon as the thirty-third state to be admitted to the Union.

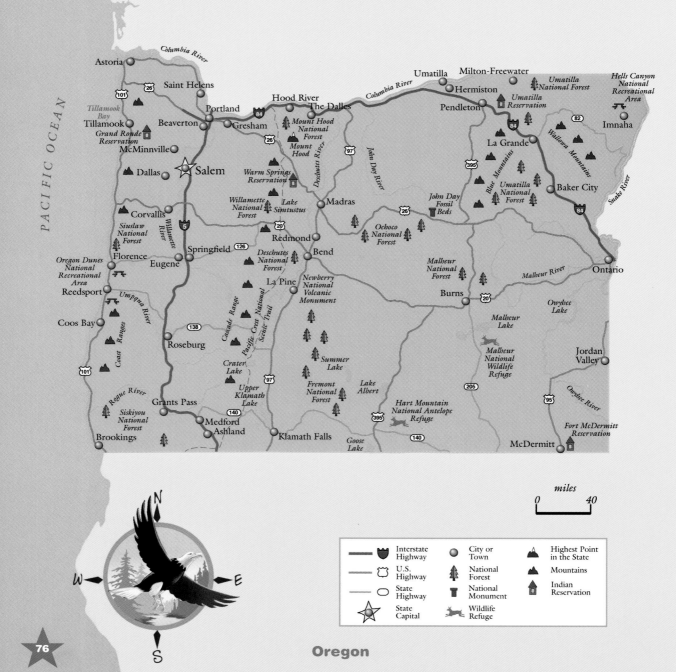

OREGON

Astoria
Saint Helens
Columbia River

101
26
Tillamook Bay
Tillamook
Grand Ronde Reservation
Beaverton
McMinnville
Portland
Gresham
Hood River
The Dalles
Columbia River
Umatilla
Milton-Freewater
Hermiston
Pendleton
Umatilla National Forest
Umatilla Reservation
Hells Canyon National Recreational Area
84
26
Mount Hood National Forest
Mount Hood
84
La Grande
395
Wallowa Mountains
82
Imnaha

PACIFIC OCEAN

Dallas
Salem
Warm Springs Reservation
Deschutes River
97
John Day River
Blue Mountains
Umatilla National Forest
Baker City
Snake River

Corvallis
Willamette National Forest
Lake Simtustus
Madras
84

Siuslaw National Forest
Willamette River
5
Springfield
126
Redmond
29
26
Ochoco National Forest
John Day Fossil Beds

Florence
Eugene
Deschutes National Forest
Bend
Malheur National Forest
Malheur River
Ontario

Oregon Dunes National Recreational Area
Reedsport
La Pine
Newberry National Volcanic Monument
Burns
20

Umpqua River
Malheur Lake

Coos Bay
Coast Ranges
138
Cascade Range
Pacific Crest National Scenic Trail
Summer Lake
Malheur National Wildlife Refuge
Owyhee Lake
Jordan Valley

Roseburg
Crater Lake
Upper Klamath Lake
97
Fremont National Forest
Lake Albert
205
Owyhee River
95

Rogue River
Grants Pass
140
Hart Mountain National Antelope Refuge
Fort McDermitt Reservation

Siskiyou National Forest
Medford
Ashland
Klamath Falls
Goose Lake
395
140

Brookings
McDermitt

miles
0   40

Legend

Interstate Highway	City or Town	Highest Point in the State		
U.S. Highway	National Forest	Mountains		
State Highway	National Monument	Indian Reservation		
State Capital	Wildlife Refuge			

N
W   E
S

Oregon

Oregon, My Oregon

Words by John Andrew Buchanan
Music by Henry Murtagh

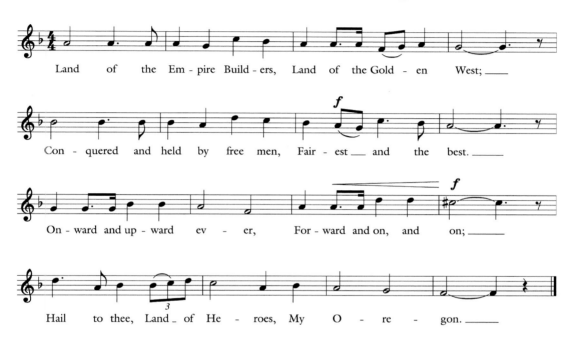

Land of the Em - pire Build - ers, Land of the Gold - en West;

Con - quered and held by free men, Fair - est and the best.

On - ward and up - ward ev - er, For - ward and on, and on;

Hail to thee, Land of He - roes, My O - re - gon.

More About Oregon

Books About the State

Boone, Mary. *Uniquely Oregon.* Chicago: Heinemann Library, 2004.

Graham, Amy. *The Oregon Trail and the Daring Journey West by Wagon.* Berkeley Heights, NJ: MyReportLinks.com Books, 2006.

Gunderson, Mary. *Oregon Trail Cooking.* Mankato, MN: Blue Earth Books, 2000.

Knapp, Ron. *Oregon.* Berkeley Heights, NJ: MyReportLinks.com Books, 2002.

Web Sites

Official State of Oregon Web Site

http://www.oregon.gov/

The Oregon Trail

http://www.isu.edu/~trinmich/Oregontrail.html

About the Author

Joyce Hart fell in love with writing while she was a student at the University of Oregon. She raised her children in Eugene and is currently a freelance writer and the author of six books. For the past twenty years she has enjoyed traveling the back roads of the Pacific Northwest.

Index

Page numbers in **boldface** are illustrations.